The Gold That Stays

Carson Pytell

Acknowledgments

Tracks .... first published in **Vita Brevis Press**

Stars .... first published in **Poetry Pacific**

Frogs .... first published in **Futures Trading**

Winds .... first published in **Squawk Back**

Physis .... first published in **Down in the Dirt Magazine**

Grass .... first published in **Futures Trading**

Loafer .... first published in **Down in the Dirt Magazine**

Burning .... first published in **Vita Brevis Press**

Playing .... first published in **Neologism Poetry Journal**

Growth .... first published in **Impspired**

Footsteps .... first published in **Vita Brevis Press**

Her .... first published in **Spillwords Press**

Badlands .... first published in **Poesis Journal**

Day .... first published in **Scarlet Leaf Review**

Oat .... first published in **Vita Brevis Press**

Dirt .... first published in **Wordgathering**

Stones .... first published in **Alien Buddha Press**

Sun .... first published in **Vita Brevis Press**

Mercies .... first published in **Scarlet Leaf Review**

Ides .... first published in **Squawk Back**

Appreciation .... first published in **POETiCA REViEW**

Caves .... first published in **Cruel Garters**

Orizaba .... first published in **Vita Brevis Press**

Airs .... first published in **Squawk Back**

Bells .... first published in **Spillwords Press**

Worms .... first published in **Vita Brevis Press**

Tracks

The old man took me into snowy woods
to fetch timber for the stove.
He, being a man, walked directly up the hill
where the timber lay covered
and immediately bent his back to it.

And I, being a child,
rolled snowballs here,
looked up trees there,
paced around my own tracks
and counted them once or twice
before beginning a snowman.

After a while father called me over,
but he didn't need any help with the logs.
We only stood quiet a moment amongst the snow
and looked back at where we came.

Then he asked if I saw anything worth seeing.
And I did, of course I did.
But I was only a child, and didn't think twice.
Now, being a man, the only difference is
I bring in the logs first.

Stars

It is said we are born of stardust,
elementally at least.
The carbon in us is out there too,
glimmering when the sun goes to rest.
And when we die our elements
head skyward and join the Heavens.
If we're lucky, to be part of a star.
But even there we cannot escape death,
even stars must collapse and die,
even if it's after millennia.
But, like our deaths becoming
food for future light,
the elements of a dead star,
maybe a little of us,
scatter and form life anew.
Seems like death, more than the end,
is the beginning of anything.

Frogs

A child's pet frog,
one caught in the nearby stream
after a chase and a few missed grabs,
then promptly put into a bucket with some water
and rushed home to a pre-prepared terrarium
with all the works: turf, stones and a crafted pond
in one corner where the frog could hydrate itself
after sitting under the articulating lamp
the child installed in his bedroom's door frame
so he could watch it eat all the flies he caught
with it's ever entertaining tongue flashes
that are so fast you'd miss them in a blink
but were always recorded just in case,
lasted about a week.

Shaky, he carried the body downstairs to his mother,
who told him to throw it as deep into the woods as he could
so the dog wouldn't find and eat it.
She threw up on the carpet last time.

Winds

Capricious they may be,
but variety is salubrious.
Things can get so boring.

In wind is possibility.
The sky and I pucker.
Here's everywhere.

Plains empty me of myself,
brother waves sympathize,
mountains match my awareness.

Nothing else, no less,
endlessly I go, caressed,
leeward over heaven.

Physis

The waking hour, sat upon a high promontory
stretching from woods over a mirrored sky.

A hearty breeze picks up, tousles matted hair,
traces a stiff chill from the neck down.

Fifty yards out is a rocky islet, one tree.
In a gaze and gape all necessary is said.

Grass

Outside my father is mowing the lawn
after a long day of work,
and I've been inside only trying to think,
trying to grow some insight
out of an infertile plot,
to cultivate a crop
I forgot to plant,
doing my best to
work just as hard
so I can sleep,
and, yet,
only my hair and fingernails grow.
How satisfying mowing must be.

Loafer

Easter, I was little,
couldn't say exactly how old,
but I was playing in the swamp
just down the road.

About five, six feet in
was a glinting turtle
lounging on a stone. I rolled
my khakis up to my knees.

But, wading in, I splashed some
and ended up scaring it off.
No big deal though.
I'd be back.

Then, on my way out of the muck,
I felt some suction at my foot
and yanked it up, leaving a
penny loafer behind.

So to this day I buy my son
only knock-arounds -
he wears them even on holidays -
and I don't mind spending all that money.

Burning

An ember of marvel crackles within,
that which drives me deep into empty pools,
down the ubiquitous tree,
even to the ground moving under the sky,
always jumping, burning at the enterprises.

If I could reach it, hold it, I'd pin it on my chest
and parade, a walking smokestack,
through world's every corner,
demonstrating as I go the immensity,
the effort, the pride in its interminability.

And should I ever grow old and infirm
and can no longer reach the pool's bottom,
the roots or even the brown lawn,
sure as death my ember still will burn,
prodded if only by darling stray memory.

Playing

Filling the terrarium with sand and stone,
a ring of water, some grass,
and amassing the insects to populate it.

Then, only then, the peace of play,
of peering in from above,
observing their small actions,
shining the lamp on them,
eventually committing cronyism
with the best behaved
and pummeling with perdition the ants;
plenty and pestilent.

Kids do the damndest things, then,
naturally as they came, but with pause,
pull the plug on them.

Growth

It was the trunks which had charm,
I could reach the caterpillars there.
One summer there were so many
you could hear them all chewing.

As usual, I spent the days
collecting and cataloging them
before they turned into butterflies
which, like treetops, are overrated.

Footsteps

One cannot always see them.
They are there,
whether distant or near:
invisible and occupying
scrolls or vellum or laminae,
or kitchen floors or family rooms
occasionally found or discovered.

If on the way through dense forest
or town or to the refrigerator,
we're always walking paths.
Some tracks sunk into mud,
some raised from marble.

Her

Shakespeare is shamed and shackled
by but a whimper of the wind.
Monet, Turner, supreme in their way,
still bow to the scaping sovereign.

Always we've worked to emulate Her -
look long into Niaux, Chauvet, Lascaux -
or at least to glean from grapes and grain -
Perses, if he listened, should be proud.

Nature, as was said, is much more
than what we see.
So, in a garden, there's no reason not
for ignominy.

Badlands

Orange hour, burdens down,
yet the things above my head;
faces I know not, names I do
and never haven't, alight me.

Of lulling roofs on rain I've dreamt,
seen horses full of themselves,
been to life and back and still
bend in hallow breezes.

For crises come bolting and blindly,
the moon is in control of the sea,
it's hard not to feel bad and work well
and there are just so many stars.

Still, night stoops cold and darkly
and, upon me, the silk I lay
drapes diaphanous yet warm enough
to cease a shivering day.

Day

The distances you reach
and infinite forms occupy,
like the spoon, sane queen and swan;
white, of golden grace, glimmering, gone.

You have places to go,
I'll stay. You're never out too long.
It's why I love the stars at night
and even more so every day.

Oat

The artist,
feeding mostly our meals,
tough but not inedible,
able to stand up to the heat
yet yielding more in the mild,
putting up with rain like a lake,
common though still a fraction
and ripe with manifold essentials;
is little else than oat
occupying a corner in the wheat.

Dirt

One needs but some dirt,
eyes to plan, hands to dig,
seeds, and the wisdom that,
with toil and time, they'll grow.

An almanac wouldn't hurt,
but remember the windows.
The garden is tacit knowledge,
less bookish than handsy.

Just to sit and scrutinize
the differences and dogmas
of all sediment and soil, is to
water grey gardens with black motor oil.

Stones

Over in Tibet,
where the Dalai Lama's from,
they call it a sky burial.
I know, but bare with me.

When a person dies
what's left is laid on stone,
compassionately,
for subsisting vultures.

They also save yak dung
to burn in their furnaces
and bask in the warm stink.
Pigeons make stool on our stone.

Sun

You know the sun is burning out, don't you?
It's dying, just very slowly. Slowly and lovely.
So slowly, in fact, one wouldn't be wrong to say it lives.
After all, distant as the death of the sun is our own,
and we don't dare call it dying when we burn.
And lovely, so lovely too, that one can't go on without it.
It wakes us, feeds meals, gives Earth something to do.
The productivity wouldn't kill, but fill our time.
If I could, I would die like the sun each day I live.

Mercies

Though tracing always the paths of voyagers past,
hoping somehow to see new waves or winds,
I, topside, posture amidst the spindrift.

Flotsam of the endeavor bobs inferentially away,
but, for its spirit sparked the journey,
jetsam I turn from seeing cast over.

Past the grasp of the gale the harbor awaits,
where I can unload my curation and redeem it,
taking whatever silver may come.

Days out now, not long for night.
When these winds have passed over
to my room at the stern I'll return and indite:

There are no ports
but for the storms.
I am at their mercies.

Ides

Longer days have more room for it.
The window divides none of the wind.
No garden better than brown.

But a bearded man comes breathing anyway,
bends with bagged hand behind his bitch
and doesn't even bat an eye.
What misappropriation!

The sun cannot be trusted.
Barren boughs break my sky.
I am small, small and delicate.

Appreciation

Without the knowledge
we are damned to
glad ingratitude.

Captives of content, we turn out
too taken, held, Stockholmed
to read what writes us.

Life does that to people.
We shape heroes and hope from stars
which spell always, everywhere:
Morte me fecit.

Caves

Earth is to sky a tether
how love loves hate some way,
and Einstein did have a couple beers
like Isadora Duncan sat down.

One in a room for a life,
but food and colors and hands,
will fingerpaint a divinity
never to come around.

Then again, the prisoner
unbound from pure perception
run back to shade's correction,
ought have been understood.

Yet the doughty doodles find
themselves unseen, unsaved, but
the frames: original, hand-carved,
gilded, are coveted, scribbled same.

And when the man, forced to see,
came back with endless yarn,
spun it into a sleeping mask,
blind again, just not for long.

Orizaba

Farther spindrift smells saltiest near,
stronger than grass whose name none think ask
because it is everywhere as unrippled reflections
of you, upon you, walking there, there and again
on green blades capped just to come back,
knowing well to not call it sailing.

Cutting such wake is to mowing the lawn
one to a song, a duty to another duty,
the difference between not the hours,
the breaks, but the breadth of seeing
birds when you hear them and
hearing them for seeing birds' sake.

Airs

Pale wayfarer, lit solely by spare
blades crept in canopy's cracks,
moves anxious, still reverently,
upon matted forest floor.

Genera of the trees he knows by now
and would usually stand and nod,
though necessarily passes posthaste,
denying heretofore critical air.

For he, in dire hopes of his own,
trains wildly toward some said glade
in which he strives to seed himself
and wait to ride what tree may grow.

Bells

Wrestling crotchety cathexes,
the objects of which are himself,
legacy and ripe ultimacy,
the carillonneur walks to work.

Solitary in morning's hush,
just his chipping steps and breath
beat their best against it,
nightingales' screech.

Reveille, he's concluded, for it is
now stark and morbidly monotonous,
will be culled today for a new song,
one to be rung loudly as possible.

Bless the carillon, the tool,
pray for the old ringer, the man
who climbs slowly now up the belfry,
hell-bent on beating the birds.

Mimesis

On a walk I saw a silvery man with an easel
focusing on the mountainscape behind me.
For kicks I sat down on a bench in his sights
and stayed there for some time, long enough.

When I got up I looped around
and snuck a look on my way past.
I saw only the mountains, the sky.
He didn't even include the bench

Worms

The wanton will have their day,
but this one is mine
to catch, capitalize, watch,
or whittle even into some trinket
someday to be displayed
in a grand cabinet of particle board,
until dusk is delivered and my glass
views a shadow unshaken
by night's odd omniscience,
for I have lived considering but life,
such sensible study,
whose dizygotic double disregards
day's duration or what's done in it,
whose duty is but inconsideration
finally to be requited,
and who leaves the rest;
kisses, laughter, memory,
in solemnity, succulence reposed.

Trees

We waded in the stream that cut through the park
looking under every rock we could find for crayfish,
drank mineral water from a spout I was still
short enough to stand underneath and drink,
then all went on a long walk past geysers,
caves, ancient boulders, on a path which led to a waterfall
where we skipped rocks in the pool that gathered at its bottom.
Packing up at the end of the day, almost ready to leave,
I found a tree small enough to wrap my arms around
and declared it to be my best friend. It made sense.
My father, upon hearing what I said, cried some
when he told my mother my best friend was a tree.
But he was wrong to cry. I didn't mean it was my only friend.
It only made sense to me to say. I laughed.
When I take the old man out on slow walks now he reminds me
of the story and laughs, looks around, inhales deep and nods.

Hills

I was out riding bikes with some friends
when they decided to go into the woods,
to a path we had only before walked on.

Their 8-speed mountain bikes navigated the terrain;
the downed trees, the rocks, roots,
and my hand-me-down beater barely kept up.

Halfway through there was a steep hill;
one dared down, then another, then my turn.
And I bit it. I dared and I failed.

And all my friends chuckled and pointed.
So I walked my bike back home
and asked dad to tend to my wound.

He poured peroxide on it, saying:
"A little pain is good for you,"
not knowing he was wrong.

Because I still wear the scar. I still ride,
but now stay on the roads.
I'll never dare hit another hill.

Roses

I used to pick roses in my grandmother's garden every Sunday we visited.
I'd use my forefinger and my thumb to carefully pinch part of the stem
where there were no thorns to prick me,
pluck the stems clean and bind them with a piece of string or cloth
then bring them inside to her. She'd always thank and kiss me.

At first it was enjoyable, but eventually I found myself bored with flowers.
The odor, their delicate petals, they grew meaningless as they did beautiful.
The familiarity of them had driven me to an apathy toward their beauty.
But still I carefully picked them, brought them in and accepted her kiss,
and she'd bring out the same vase as every time and put them in it.

One Sunday, late in summer, as I was kneeling once again in the garden,
I absentmindedly pinched part of a stem where a thorn was.
The blood trickled out of the tip of my thumb, crimson and glistening,
and an epiphanic spark ran from my skull to my feet
when I wiped my blood on a petal.

Without plucking the thorns off or even binding the flowers together this time
I ran inside and presented my grandmother her newest bouquet.
When she grabbed them she shouted and went to the kitchen sink
to pluck the thorns out of her palm and wash the blood off.
Soon as she was done she kicked my behind. I knew I was on to something.

Cartography

Mapping majestic minutiae
means work:
daily the same clothes,
thin at knee and elbow,
the same vocation
to hold and haul;
studying the same stones
under different suns,
the growth of the grass
on any given day,
the movement of mountains,
every momentous millimeter,
bringing to light where borders lie,
and bridges too,
and noting, always noting,
how any second of this
can occupy a life.

9 789390 601615